Brodsworth Hall and Gardens

Caroline Carr-Whitworth

Introduction

Brodsworth Hall is a remarkable example of a mid-Victorian country house that survives as an ensemble, with many of its original contents and surrounding gardens.

The house and gardens were the creation of one man, Charles Sabine Augustus Thellusson, in one decade, the 1860s. He had inherited the Brodsworth estate of 8,000 acres (3,240 hectares) in 1859, after half a century of legal dispute over the family inheritance. He completely remodelled the estate to create a country seat to suit his family's needs, his appetite for country pursuits and his position among Yorkshire's landed classes. The new Brodsworth Hall was conservative in taste, richly furnished and with a well-organized service wing for the numerous staff required to run it.

After Charles Sabine Augustus Thellusson's death in 1885 the Brodsworth estate, by then bringing a diminishing income, was inherited by each of his four sons in turn. In 1931 the estate passed to his grandson, Charles Grant-Dalton, for whose daughter, Pamela, it was then held in trust from 1952. This was a time when many country houses were being abandoned, but Charles Grant-Dalton's widow, Sylvia, valiantly continued to live at the hall for over 30 years, supported by ever fewer staff. By the time of her death, in 1988, Brodsworth faced an uncertain future as Pamela, then Mrs Williams, did not wish to live in the house. In 1990 Mrs Williams gave the house and gardens to English Heritage, and they were opened to the public in 1995.

Brodsworth's interiors have been gently conserved to show how subsequent generations lived with Thellusson's creation, updating or abandoning parts of the house to suit their needs and means. The gardens have been restored to recapture the spirit of the 1860s, while retaining traces of both earlier and later elements.

Above: Charles Sabine Augustus Thellusson (1822–85) with his wife Georgiana and one of their children. Little evidence survives about Georgiana's life or her role in the creation of Brodsworth

Facing page: The inner hall, where the most impressive of Brodsworth's 19th-century Italian marble statues stand out against the colourful decoration

Tour of the Hall

Charles Sabine Augustus Thellusson's Brodsworth Hall was intended for family life, which included the entertainment of relations and guests. The hall combines grandeur, comfort and an efficient layout, having impressive reception rooms, circulation spaces and an extensive servants' wing. Its design and furnishings reflect the conservative taste and sense of social hierarchy that was typical of the landed gentry of the mid-Victorian period.

Over the years the family made many alterations to the interiors, which had become increasingly faded and worn. The conservation of the hall's interiors aims to arrest their decay as far as possible, and to show how a Victorian country house survived and was lived in until the late 20th century.

FOLLOWING THE TOUR

The tour takes visitors from the visitor centre to the front door and then through the family and servants' quarters. The small numbered plans in the margins highlight the key plans in the tour.

MAIN DRIVE AND ENTRANCE

Visitors to Brodsworth Hall come up the main drive, which was laid out in the 1860s as the approach to the new house, through the park. From the visitor centre, a gateway leads into the pleasure gardens surrounding the house. The 18th-century stone gate piers are among the many elements from the earlier Brodsworth Hall that Thellusson reused as part of his new house.

The drive sweeps up to the main entrance, which has a columned porte cochère where travellers could alight from a carriage under cover. The T-shaped plan of the hall can be seen clearly: the tall family block stretches behind the entrance on the short east front, with all the principal rooms looking out from the long south front over the park. The servants' wing adjoins the main block at right angles and set back from it, reflecting the separate but interlinked communities of family and staff in a Victorian country house. The servants' wing reuses 18th-century windows and stonework from the earlier hall. It would have been screened from view by shrubs, which have been replanted.

Thellusson's new house was built between 1861 and 1863 to the design of a minor London architect, Philip Wilkinson, using white magnesian limestone quarried on the estate. Its restrained Italianate style was a safe, rather conservative choice for country houses in the mid-19th century. It has minimal classical detailing, with urns on the balustrade and slight variations in the window surrounds. Its façades are rigidly symmetrical, so a few of the windows are false, not being needed by the interior plan. The architecture and the immediate setting, with lawns and statuary in a matching formal Italianate style, provided Thellusson with a house quietly expressive of his solid wealth and cultivated taste.

Brodsworth
Hall

Visitor centre

Above: The porte cochère
photographed in the 1870s
Below: The contrasting scale
of the family and servants'
wings seen from the east
Facing page: Nymph
Going to Bathe by Giuseppe
Lazzerini (1831–95)

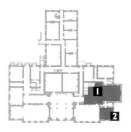

◗ ENTRANCE HALL AND INNER HALL

The entrance hall was designed for the bustle of arrival and departure. Doors on one side led to a vestibule for coats and a water closet, and on the other gave the butler easy access from the servants' wing to the front door.

The eye is immediately drawn from the shadowy intimacy of the entrance to the magnificent full-height and top-lit inner hall, where marble sculptures stand out brightly against the main stairs. A curtained archway to the side frames a view through a series of further halls. The logical house plan allows discreet points where servants could gain access to the rooms for their work.

The entrance and inner halls set the tone and character of the house, combining impressive circulation spaces with a degree of comfort given by the plush carpets and curtains, which screen out draughts and provide privacy. The visual unity of Brodsworth's interiors was achieved in great part through the work of Lapworth Brothers, the smart London furnishing firm that supplied the mahogany furniture, matching textile hangings, upholstery and carpets throughout the house in 1863.

The halls are in keeping with the Italianate style of the exterior, but with strongly contrasting colours and textures. The columns and pilasters are made of scagliola, or imitation marble, in three colours: red, yellow and a brilliant white on the upper stairs. The walls are painted and varnished to form panels and borders that also resemble coloured marbles. The predominantly crimson and gold scheme is picked up by the carpets, curtains and Minton tiles. In contrast to all this colour are the many sculptures in Italian marble, bought by Thellusson in 1865 to complete the scheme.

Below: The entrance hall, looking towards the inner hall, with a glimpse of halls beyond. The largest white marble statue is Education *by Giuseppe Lazzerini, at the foot of the stairs*

Above: Sylvia and Charles Grant-Dalton in the morning room in the 1930s, shortly before the fireplace was altered

Left: The morning room today. Brodsworth's fragile interiors have been conserved as far as possible as they were found

2 MORNING ROOM

This room would have been used initially for family business: for the mistress to give her instructions to the housekeeper, or the master to deal with his agent. Its small scale meant that it continued to be used over the years as a family sitting room.

The changes made by each generation can be seen overlaying the original faded, Victorian furnishing scheme. The wallpaper – imitating stamped-leather wall-hangings – and most of the furniture survive from the 1860s, although damaged by damp, light and insects. Their condition has been stabilized as far as possible.

An equestrian portrait of Charles Sabine Augustus Thellusson hangs over the fireplace, surrounded by paintings of family dogs, some painted by his daughter Aline in the 1870s, and four commissioned from artist W H Trood (1848–99) in the 1890s by Thellusson's eldest son, Peter, and Peter's wife, Elizabeth.

The electric light fitting dates from 1913, when Charles Thellusson, the third son, replaced gas with electricity. He and his wife Constance Mary also updated the decoration in many rooms, and bought this red carpet for a bedroom; it was brought into the morning room by Charles and Sylvia Grant-Dalton when they were trying to make the house more comfortable in the 1930s. They also reduced the size of the fireplace opening to make the fire burn more efficiently. The family resorted to an electric fire in the later 20th century when there were fewer servants to carry coal and clean grates.

3 DINING ROOM

Thellusson's dining room, hung with his most important paintings and comfortably furnished with a mahogany table and red leather chairs from Lapworths, provided an impressive setting for the family meals and entertaining that were so central to country-house life. The large double portrait of Thellusson's grandmother and father as a small boy by the eminent society painter Sir Thomas Lawrence (1769–1830) illustrates the route by which the Thellusson fortune was inherited, enabling this house to be built.

The other portraits in the room, and all the Dutch paintings, came from his wife Georgiana's family, the Theobalds, reflecting the contribution of her inheritance, too. Her grandfather, John Theobald, depicted over the fireplace, bred and raced horses. His most prestigious trophy, the

Right: The dining room
Below: The menu for Charles and Constance Mary Thellusson's silver-wedding celebrations in 1910

Facing page, above: Sylvia Grant-Dalton in front of The 'Dolphin' off Amsterdam by Ludolf Backhuysen (c.1631–1708)
Facing page, bottom: The dining-room table laid for the 1910 silver-wedding party

1835 Goodwood Cup, sits on the sideboard between two of Thellusson's yachting trophies. In pride of place above these, in an alcove specially designed for it, hangs *The 'Dolphin' off Amsterdam*, painted in the 1660s by the renowned maritime painter Ludolf Backhuysen (c.1631–1708). This was the most important of the six Dutch paintings that Thellusson purchased in 1850 at the sale of the extensive collection of his late father-in-law, William Theobald. Four of the other

Dutch paintings used to hang with the family portraits, but their number has sadly diminished over the years. Portraits of Georgiana and her sister by Margaret Carpenter (1793–1872) flank the Backhuysen.

The design of the house, with the kitchen at the junction of the servants' and family wings, meant that staff had a short journey to carry food from a hatch at the back of the kitchen, through a door concealed in the panelling of the corridor, and to the sideboard. The crimson portière curtains may have been pulled across the archways to hide the awkward traversing of the family corridor by the servants.

The dining room continued in regular use, with Mrs Grant-Dalton eating on her own and entertaining here until her death in 1988. Because of such heavy use, there have been repairs and alterations. Charles and Constance Mary Thellusson replaced the crimson carpet with the present blue one in 1904. Blue curtains were provided to match in the 1970s as the original crimson velvet ones, of which a tiny reminder remains on the shelf under the Lawrence portrait, had become brown and weakened by the sun.

'Mr Charles Thellusson [above] always liked his meat cooked thoroughly, but the cook, Martha Lockey, was determined it was going to be done properly, which was "rare". And there used to be such a roar from the dining room, followed by the leg of whatever it was. The kitchen maid Caroline got rather sick of this, so when Martha went to have a rest in the afternoons, Caroline would pop the beef back in the oven to see that it was well done. And then there was no roar coming out of the dining room after that.'
Christina Edwards recalls memories of her mother-in-law Caroline Palmer, kitchen maid then cook, 1906 to 1916

Right: The decorative scheme of the main halls continues in the south hall. In the foreground is Vanity by Giuseppe Lazzerini

Below: This 1902 Monarch gramophone provided a fashionable and expensive form of entertainment

4 SOUTH HALL

The south hall was primarily a circulation space designed to impress. It was the midpoint of the 'dinner route' from drawing room to dining room and gave access to the south terrace. Its wall silks, mirrors and seat furniture matched those of the drawing room. The yellow Siena scagliola columns and marble statues would have stood out against the crimson of the original silk wall-coverings. These were replaced with yellow silk in the early 20th century by Charles and Constance Mary Thellusson. The marble fire surround and mahogany doors, with their sculptural ornamental 'overdoors', came from the 18th-century Brodsworth Hall. Many elements from this earlier hall were economically reused in the new house, to which their classical style was well matched.

The south hall provided a space that could be used informally as a sitting room or music room. A series of magnificent gramophones and an American organ were to be found here in the days when Charles and Constance Mary often had younger members of the family staying.

5 BILLIARD ROOM

The furnishings and paintings in this room are particularly evocative of the sporting interests of the men of the family. A billiard room was standard in Victorian country houses. It is located neatly in the central T-junction of the house, next door to the kitchen, since top-lighting was suitable for both rooms. The massive table, cues and scoreboard came from the specialist supplier Cox & Yemen of London. Benches raised on platforms were provided by Lapworths, in the buttoned red-leather upholstery reminiscent of gentlemen's clubs and much favoured at Brodsworth.

Frequent use meant that many repairs and improvements were made over the years. In the 1880s the present Silentium linoleum and red carpet on the platform replaced the originals from Lapworths, and two ventilation shafts were fitted, probably to help remove cigar smoke. The benches were reupholstered at the turn of the century, and the Grant-Daltons painted the walls blue in the 1930s, replacing an earlier muted-red scheme.

The magnificent early 19th-century paintings of horses were almost all inherited by Georgiana Thellusson. Some are of horses owned and bred by her grandfather, notably the mares and foals in *The Theobald Stud* by James Barenger (1780–1831) hanging over the fireplace. John Theobald himself

can be seen to the right of the scoreboard, depicted by James Ward (1769–1859), with his most successful racehorse, Rockingham, and the jockey Jem Robinson, in the year of their victory at Goodwood in 1835. Ward's portraits of famous racehorses either side of the fireplace and opposite the door were probably acquired for his collection by John's son, William Theobald. To the left of the scoreboard is *Rataplan* by Harry Hall (c.1814–82), a horse bred from the Theobald stud and which came to be owned by Charles Sabine Augustus Thellusson's father. He raced the horse hard, often relying on its winnings in his regular periods of financial insecurity.

Over the door is a portrait of Peter Thellusson, eldest son of Charles Sabine Augustus Thellusson. While his father had commissioned some of the fastest and biggest sailing yachts of the day, Peter preferred steam, and is depicted here on board his steam yacht *Albion* by artist George Percy Jacomb-Hood (1857–1929).

Above: This tinted porcelain figurine, probably made in Germany in about 1900, is a risqué addition to the room
Below: Paintings of racehorses, including four by the admired animal painter James Ward (1769–1859), look down from the walls of the billiard room

6

Below: The drawing room in the 1880s, showing the protective chintz coverings for the furniture and the unfaded carpet and textiles

Facing page: The drawing room as it is today

'*I can remember two hunt balls because of the upheaval. The first one, we were all told to get down with rags on our feet and polish. The drawing room is a very big room to polish by foot, I can tell you. And it was splintered beyond belief. The next "do", they hired a floor, but it didn't quite fit – there was a little gap round the edge' Pamela Williams (née Grant-Dalton), speaking in 1993*

6 DRAWING ROOM

This room was designed on a grand scale but in a light decorative style. It was used, especially by the women of the family, to entertain visitors making afternoon calls, and family and guests before and after dinner.

The decorative scheme created by Lapworths in 1863 for Georgiana Thellusson was once vibrantly coloured. Its style was loosely based on 18th-century French interiors, with decorative giltwood frames to the wall panels, mirrors and pelmets. Three different designs of crimson silk were used for the walls, window drapery and reupholstery of an 18th-century set of giltwood seating and the mid-19th-century central ottoman. Lapworths' 'Extra Superfine Real Axminster' hand-knotted carpet for this room was, at £367.10s, the most expensive the firm provided for the whole house. Lapworths also supplied items by other manufacturers, such as the 24-light 'large handsome Glass Chandelier in the Venetian style for Gas', and its slightly smaller counterpart, probably made by the famous Victorian manufacturer Perrys.

The ceiling, the most elaborate in the hall, is delicately painted with floral swags, and putti (cherubs) and emblems relating to the arts and the seasons, drawing on Renaissance decoration.

Musical instruments in the corners of the ceiling of the smaller section of the room, which is separated slightly by white scagliola columns, indicates its use for music. The Broadwood grand piano, with its rosewood case and iron frame, was bought in 1855 for Georgiana and was brought from the Thellussons' house in Brighton in 1866.

Changes in the way the room was used over the years have affected its appearance. Although it continued to be used for large occasions such as hunt balls and charity events, and formally by Mrs Grant-Dalton on Sundays, it gradually lost some of its original contents. Sunlight from its five full-length south-facing windows has greatly faded the drawing-room textiles and woodwork, particularly once the protective sun curtains, blinds and chintz covers from Lapworths were no longer used. Examples of these highly decorative glazed-cotton covers, of which two full sets were supplied for this room and for the south hall, can be seen on the two side chairs by the columns.

The Grant-Daltons preferred to use an upstairs room as a sitting room, taking the carpet from the smaller section of this room (which is now therefore slightly less faded) and shortening all the drawing-room curtains to fit the upstairs room. Just the pelmets were left behind, as a reminder of the room's once more opulent appearance.

Right: The view back from the west hall, through three pairs of portière curtains towards a sculpture in the entrance hall
Below: Panels and borders along each wall were painted to resemble coloured marbles

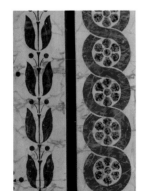

7 WEST HALL

The furnishing of the hallways comes to a climax in the west hall, with marbling, stencilling, gilding and densely grouped sculptures multiplied infinitely by opposing mirrors. The space is gently lit with light borrowed from the library through an internal window of opaque glass, its edges richly painted with seasonal fruits and cherubic scenes.

Sleep of Innocence by Giosuè Argenti (1819–1901) takes the central position, back-lit by the window. On either side are pairs of figures evoking supposed feminine virtues; *Fidelity* and *Application* by Pietro Franchi (1817–78) react

differently to their little dogs, while Biblical motherhood is depicted in a marble version of a Raphael painting of the Virgin Mary, and in *Eve*, or *The First Cradle*, after a work by French sculptor Auguste-Hyacinthe Debay (1804–65).

A large version of the *Venus de' Medici*, once regarded as the epitome of beauty, faces the main approach to the female stronghold of the drawing room. That room itself used to contain three sculptures of female figures set in front of the mirrors between its windows. After one of these, and another small sculpture, were sold at auction in 1947, the other two were moved out into the nearby north hall.

Sculpture at Brodsworth

Brodsworth's large group of 19th-century sculpture is one of its most memorable features, an important part of the original vision for the Italianate house and garden. In filling Brodsworth with sculpture, Charles Sabine Augustus Thellusson was following the tradition of country-house owners for whom sculpture had long been a mark of cultural and social prestige. His collection also reflects the appeal in the mid-19th century for art which, as well as loosely evoking the classical world, idealized femininity, often in a sentimental and coyly sensuous way, and was executed with a high level of craftsmanship.

Most of Brodsworth's sculptures are by north Italian sculptors, who at the time led the field for work with such qualities. The sensuous *Swinging Girl* by Pietro Magni (1817–77) in the entrance hall is the most technically accomplished in the house, although the most prominent position there was given to *Education*, or *Lord's Prayer* by Giuseppe Lazzerini (1831–95), a more serious expression of women's nurturing and domestic role.

Thellusson bought all the interior sculptures at the Dublin International Exhibition of 1865. While Brodsworth was largely furnished by this date, the generous spacing of the halls suggests it was intended to take sculpture from the first. All but two of Thellusson's 17 large figures and eight small

ones by a variety of sculptors were bought from one exhibitor, Chevalier Casentini, from Lucca in Tuscany. He was then paid to transport and install them on their grey marble plinths at Brodsworth in 1866. Casentini then supplied the marble statues, steps, urns, greyhounds and fountain for the gardens. Two undated drawings signed by Casentini suggest that he was emboldened to try to sell more sculpture to such a good client; they show Brodsworth Hall with pediments peppered with sculptures and a conservatory, or winter garden, where further sculptures could have been displayed – additions that were never carried out. These drawings, and the stylistic unity of the house and sculpture, led to Casentini long being credited as the architect of Brodsworth. The estate accounts show that he was in fact paid in full for 'marble works' in 1867, well after Wilkinson was paid his commission as architect in 1863.

The survival of Brodsworth's sculpture collection in the setting for which it was acquired is remarkable. As taste turned against the Victorian, such large-scale and sentimental works were often disposed of; the Grant-Daltons tried with little success to sell several in 1947. Sylvia Grant-Dalton found them not to her taste, calling them 'poor cold ladies' – an irony, given that she often found herself 'freezy-frozy cold' in the draughty house.

'Nobody knew how to clean the statues – the recipe was a secret of the housekeeper, Miss Langton. They found it when she died, and Mrs Grant-Dalton had it analysed, but it eventually got lost. It took two hours per statue – the whole day to do the big ones. The stuff we used was like a liquid paste, and we had several types of brushes to work into the ladies' curls – all the nooks and crannies. Then we swilled them down with cold water.'
Gladys Jones (née Phillips), kitchen maid then housemaid between 1935 and 1945

Above: *Jane Langton, who between 1895 and 1936 served as housemaid, lady's maid and then housekeeper at Brodsworth*
From far left: *Garden statue of one of the Muses; Application by Pietro Franchi; Swinging Girl by Pietro Magni; Franchi's Fidelity*

The Thellusson and Grant-Dalton Families

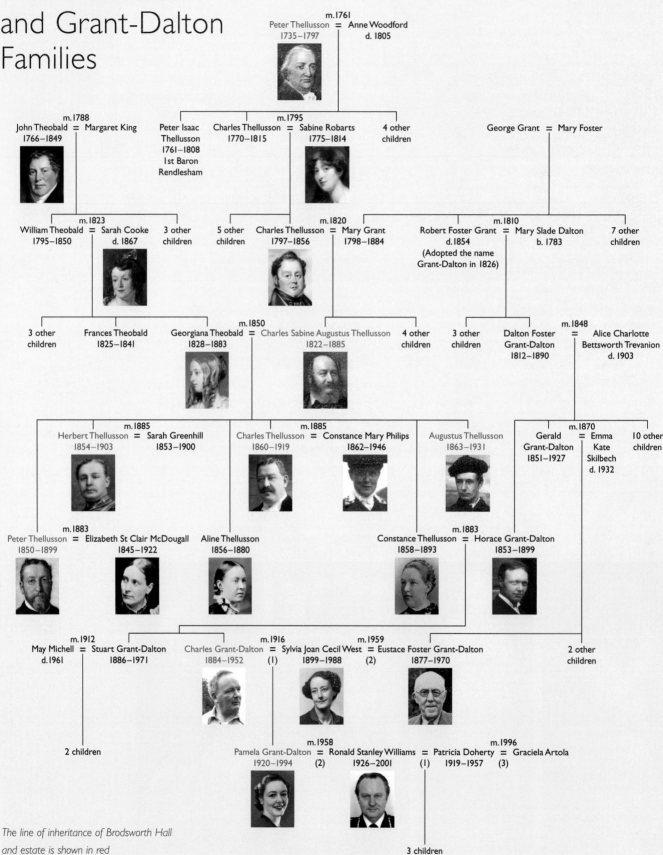

m.1761
Peter Thellusson = Anne Woodford
1735–1797   d. 1805

m.1788
John Theobald = Margaret King
1766–1849

Peter Isaac Thellusson
1761–1808
1st Baron Rendlesham

m.1795
Charles Thellusson = Sabine Robarts
1770–1815   1775–1814

4 other children

George Grant = Mary Foster

m.1823
William Theobald = Sarah Cooke
1795–1850   d. 1867

3 other children

5 other children

m.1820
Charles Thellusson = Mary Grant
1797–1856   1798–1884

m.1810
Robert Foster Grant = Mary Slade Dalton
d. 1854   b. 1783
(Adopted the name Grant-Dalton in 1826)

7 other children

3 other children

Frances Theobald
1825–1841

m.1850
Georgiana Theobald = Charles Sabine Augustus Thellusson
1828–1883   1822–1885

4 other children

3 other children

Dalton Foster Grant-Dalton
1812–1890

m.1848
= Alice Charlotte Bettsworth Trevanion
d. 1903

m.1885
Herbert Thellusson = Sarah Greenhill
1854–1903   1853–1900

m.1885
Charles Thellusson = Constance Mary Philips
1860–1919   1862–1946

Augustus Thellusson
1863–1931

Gerald Grant-Dalton
1851–1927

m.1870
= Emma Kate Skilbech
d. 1932

10 other children

m.1883
Peter Thellusson = Elizabeth St Clair McDougall
1850–1899   1845–1922

Aline Thellusson
1856–1880

m.1883
Constance Thellusson = Horace Grant-Dalton
1858–1893   1853–1899

m.1912
May Michell = Stuart Grant-Dalton
d. 1961   1886–1971

m.1916
Charles Grant-Dalton = Sylvia Joan Cecil West = Eustace Foster Grant-Dalton
1884–1952   (1)   1899–1988   (2)   1877–1970

m.1959

2 other children

2 children

m.1958
Pamela Grant-Dalton = Ronald Stanley Williams = Patricia Doherty = Graciela Artola
1920–1994   (2)   1926–2001   (1)   1919–1957   (3)

m.1996

3 children

The line of inheritance of Brodsworth Hall and estate is shown in red

16

8 LIBRARY

The books in this room take up remarkably little space, suggesting that the Thellussons' leisure interests lay elsewhere. The room's intimate scale meant that it continued in use as a comfortable sitting room. The Grant-Daltons had its fireplace opening reduced, as they did in the similar-sized morning room, and Mrs Grant-Dalton continued to use the room as her principal sitting room to the end of her life, keeping it warm with a log fire.

Most of the thousand or so books on the shelves date from the 18th century and are the remainder of a larger library belonging to Peter Thellusson, the London financier who bought the Brodsworth estate from the earls of Kinnoull in 1791. His mother can be seen in the fine portrait over the fireplace by the French artist Nicolas de Largillière (1656–1746), dating from 1725. The surviving books are typical of an 18th-century gentleman's library, and include classical authors, history and many works in French, such as the long row of volumes of Diderot's Encyclopaedia on the lower shelves. Subsequent generations of the family added a few volumes and also kept books elsewhere in the house.

The library has the same design of wallpaper as the morning room, although in a different selection of colours and in slightly

better condition. Much of the furniture here is earlier than the 1860s house and may have been inherited from either the Thellussons or Theobalds. The rosewood Pembroke table between the windows and circular table matches a pair of card tables in the drawing room by Seddon, a fashionable Regency London furniture-maker whose labels can be found on nine pieces at Brodsworth. The Grecian mahogany chairs, with their swept-back legs and carved backs, are also fine examples of early 19th-century furniture.

Top: Sylvia Grant-Dalton's desk and chair
Above: A detail from the painted border of the internal window between the library and the west hall
Left: The library in 1910, with a gas light and loose covers in a rose-patterned cretonne introduced in 1904

9

Facing page: The lathe room has been the repository for an extraordinary assortment of discarded objects for many decades

Below: Photographs on the lift-shaft wall of Mrs Grant-Dalton's family, friends, special occasions, pets and scenes around Brodsworth. Among them are the wedding of Bernadette Williams and Elie Eskenazi in 1974 (far left), Brodsworth school in its centenary year in 1971 (top centre) and some of Mrs Grant-Dalton's charitable activities (towards the bottom)

9 WATER CLOSET, NORTH HALL, LATHE ROOM, LIFT AND WEST STAIRS

Next to the library is one of the two principal water closets provided on the ground floor of the main block (of nine WCs throughout the house). It still has its original mahogany bench seat and curved marble-topped washstand. Mrs Grant-Dalton found it useful for flower-arranging, but often blocked the drain with flower stems – to the frustration of the estate foreman, Les Trott.

The last in the sequence of family rooms was initially just called the 'large spare room'. It became known as 'Captain Thellusson's Lathe Room', as Charles Sabine Augustus Thellusson enjoyed wood-turning, which had long been an acceptable hobby for gentlemen as long as they produced decorative rather than functional items. Sadly, none of his creations or equipment, which included a mahogany and brass lathe, remain in the house. The room was later used as a storeroom for garden tools and games.

Over the years the lathe room has accumulated a bizarre and fascinating mix of objects, including a great number of Victorian stuffed birds and animals, some by local taxidermists. Once spread throughout the house, these were gathered here by Mrs Grant-Dalton, who disliked them.

The sequence of halls ends with the round-headed window of the north hall, in front of which is a marble statue of a shepherdess, framed by the last of the set of crimson curtains by Lapworths. On the right is a group of three sentimental paintings of rural children by a mid-19th-century artist called William Perry. One is dated 1861, the year that building work started on the hall, so these could be among the few new paintings bought for the house.

The west stairs, considerably simpler than the main stairs, lead up from here to the lesser family bedrooms. In 1951, towards the end of Charles Grant-Dalton's life, a lift was installed for him by knocking through the wall into the housemaid's store cupboard. Visitors using the lift catch a passing glimpse of the enormous collage of family photographs and cards with which Mrs Grant-Dalton decorated the shaft's walls to amuse herself in the hours she spent stuck in the lift waiting to be hand-winched to safety by Les Trott.

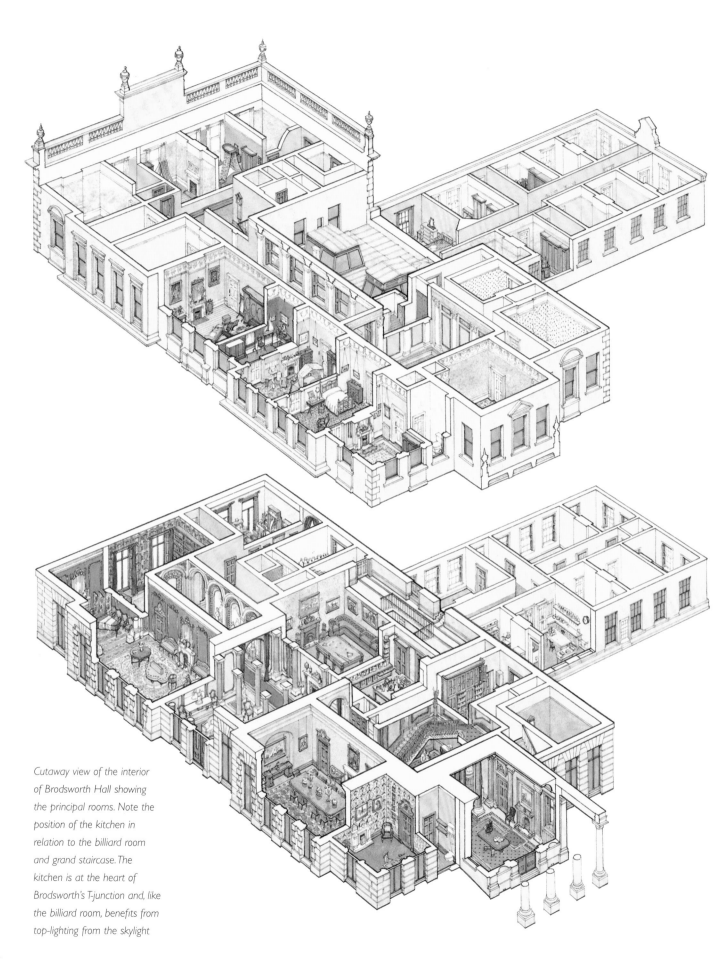

Cutaway view of the interior of Brodsworth Hall showing the principal rooms. Note the position of the kitchen in relation to the billiard room and grand staircase. The kitchen is at the heart of Brodsworth's T-junction and, like the billiard room, benefits from top-lighting from the skylight

Decay and Conservation

When English Heritage took the property on in 1990, the condition of the building's structure and interiors presented many challenges. The family undertook repairs and redecorations at intervals, but several factors, in addition to the simple passage of time, had taken their toll on Brodsworth Hall and its contents. As the numbers of estate and house staff dwindled, maintenance had been reduced. Subsidence, as a result of expanding production at the nearby Brodsworth Main Colliery, had caused cracks and problems with the way the roofs drained.

The interiors had been badly affected by water seeping in through the leaking roof and down-pipes, while damp had been rising through the walls. Further damage has been caused by insect infestation and sunlight pouring through the huge Victorian plate-glass windows.

Five years' work was required before Brodsworth could be opened to the public, and its conservation and development continues. The house had to be made watertight, and its leaking roof repaired. The soft limestone, badly affected by pollution and erosion, was cleaned, repaired and in many places, such as the columns of the porte cochère, replaced. The new stone at the base of the main façades indicates the level of rising damp caused when the 'French drains' (open trenches beneath flagstone coverings) became blocked.

Inside the house, the 1860s interiors had lost much of their vibrancy and had been altered and added to by later occupants. Their delicate condition, and an appreciation that their decay and alteration was part of the history of the house, led to the decision to conserve the interiors as they survived, rather than restore them, so as to acknowledge the losses and additions. Painstaking work was undertaken to clean and stabilize the decoration and furnishings, as far as possible without renewing or recreating lost elements. Flaking paint was reattached, and deteriorating textiles were secured with protective netting. As a result, the fragile interiors have a well-worn and gently dilapidated air, redolent of the changes in country-house life over a century.

The redecorations, repairs, deterioration and abandonment of some rooms are all part of the history of the family and staff and their lives at Brodsworth, as are the introduction for example of electric lighting or the Aga cooker in the servants' wing. They show how those living in country houses responded to the challenges and opportunities that confronted them, particularly in the late 19th and 20th centuries.

'We used to have to go on the roof after very bad snow (more than a foot) and shovel it off, because the hall used to leak so much it would just run off the roof and filter through all the slates. So if we knew the weather was going to be bad, the first job in the morning was to go straight to the hall – everybody, up through the hall, up on to the roof, and shovel it all off. We'd all have to go – the whole of the estate's workers. That was the priority. Cold, but fun.'

Les Trott, estate foreman from 1974

Above: *Restoration of the balustrade on the roof in 1991*
Above left: *The effect of a leaking down-pipe on a corner of the drawing room*
Left: *Brodsworth under a false roof during structural repairs*

⑩ BEDROOM CORRIDOR

At the top of the west stairs is the wide L-shaped corridor that gives access to all the rooms used by the family on the first floor. At this end is the only bathroom originally provided in the house, and bedrooms used by the older children and guests. Servants used the narrow stairs at each end of the corridor. Sinks and a capacious linen cupboard were nearby. As the corridor leads around the corner to more important bedrooms and dressing rooms, its decoration becomes more ornate, with scagliola pilasters and a painted dado.

⑪ FAMILY BEDROOMS

These rooms were comfortably furnished in the 1860s, with solid brown furniture supplied by Lapworths, or furniture dating from the 18th and early 19th centuries. Each room or suite of rooms was given a unified scheme by Lapworths' curtains, covers and plump upholstery in light floral chintzes. The bedroom furnishings reflected the Victorian sense of hierarchy. In contrast to the hand-knotted Axminster carpets downstairs, several grades of machine-woven Brussels carpets were provided upstairs. The corridor carpet (now a reproduction) was a scaled-down version

of the star design throughout the main halls. The principal bedrooms were given new fireplaces, while Georgian marble ones from the old hall were reused in the west bedrooms.

Initially the soft furnishings were renewed frequently, especially on the arrival of each new master and mistress of the house. As the size of the family decreased, the bedrooms were not all used regularly, and some were closed altogether in the mid-20th century. As a result, the bedrooms reveal several layers of furnishings and use. Occasionally the faded remains of a room's first scheme can be spotted on a chair or set of bed steps.

All the doors have their original dark wood-graining on the side facing the corridor, but were later painted white inside, as were most of the mahogany curtain poles and shutters. No Victorian wallpaper survives, and the bedrooms were painted in plain colours by the Grant-Daltons. The plumbed-in washbasins and abandoned hot-water jugs reflect the long struggle to operate in a house built in an era of plentiful servants. A modern bathroom has replaced one of the original water-closets at the end of the master and mistress's suite of rooms.

Right: Bedroom 14 retains the bedhangings and carpet from about 1900
Below: Constance Thellusson in the same bedroom in about 1882. This photograph shows the room's chintz chair covers and long-lost wallpaper

⟦12⟧ THE PRINCIPAL GUEST ROOM

This room at the central point of the corridor was originally furnished lavishly, with chintz curtains over the massive boat-shaped bed, or *lit en bateau*, of about the 1850s. The room fell out of use in the 20th century, but the delicate wallpaper of 1904 remains. Next to this is the suite of rooms used by the master and mistress of the house. The bedrooms, flanked by dressing rooms, open on to the landing above the main stairs. Mrs Grant-Dalton reused curtains and carpets from all over the house in these rooms.

⟦13⟧ NURSERIES AND SERVICE STAIRS

The education room, just before the main landing, has resources for the use of all visitors. This spacious room over the entrance hall was once the day nursery. Its commanding position meant that it was used by subsequent mistresses of the house as an upstairs sitting room, or 'boudoir', and its original furnishings and toys do not survive.

Returning along the main landing, under the domed skylight (partly shattered by an anti-aircraft gun in the Second World War), visitors leave the bedroom corridor past a small water closet. A pair of baize-covered doors, to deaden any noise, leads to the plainer area behind the main staircase allocated to the children and their servants. A corridor on the right leads to the governess's bedroom (now containing an exhibition about the servants), another water closet and the night nursery for the younger children. The day nursery was accessible from this corridor, and a narrow staircase led down to the schoolroom by the front door, and up to the roof for maintenance. These rooms, prone to damp, fell out of use, and have been converted for administrative purposes.

The short flight of stairs was the main route for the servants to the family bedrooms. Near the baize doors is a lead-lined sink for emptying hip-baths, wash bowls and cleaning buckets. At the bottom of the stairs another baize door separated the servants' quarters from the family.

Above: The principal guest room now has an abandoned air, having been closed by the Grant-Daltons
Left: A page from a family album. Bedrooms were provided for Charles Sabine Augustus and Georgiana Thellusson's six children, as well as for guests

Servants at Brodsworth

When the First World War broke out, there were an estimated 1.3 million domestic servants in Britain, making domestic service the biggest provider of jobs, just ahead of agriculture. An efficient staff was crucial for the running of large houses and to support the leisured lives of their owners. Most of the indoor servants at Brodsworth were women: they had the necessary skills and, in the days before equal pay, were cheaper to employ than men. A butler, valet and footmen, however, were considered essential. Until 1914, there were about 15 indoor staff at Brodsworth, including four housemaids, three kitchen maids, a scullery maid, a still-room maid and a lady's maid. Outdoors, most of the staff were men – gardeners, gamekeepers, coachmen and, from the 1910s, drivers.

The service wing also accommodated the servants of visiting guests, who slept on folding wooden beds. Female staff occupied the first-floor rooms. Separated by a flight of stairs and further service rooms, to ensure there was no impropriety, the male staff occupied the ground-floor rooms, now the shop and tea rooms.

The household staff were organised in a strict hierarchy under the authority of the butler, housekeeper and cook. The housekeeper's accounts books list monthly payments to servants in order of rank, and even their bedlinen was graded by sex and position. With diligence and hard work, however, servants or maids could work their way up the ranks. Emily Chester started as a 'garden girl' in about 1910, becoming a housemaid in 1921 and in 1936 becoming cook/housekeeper for 45 years.

When the family were away during the summer, staff received 'board wages', or half pay. During this time, staff spring-cleaned the hall, but otherwise enjoyed a lighter workload. For a select few, accompanying the family on their sailing trips provided a rare and exciting opportunity to travel.

Between the wars, the number of indoor staff fell to six, with daily help from two local women. New labour-saving equipment did ease the burden of housework, however, and housemaids recalled the luxury of having a Hoover in the 1930s, although the electricity supply from the estate generator was erratic. Washing was sent out to a commercial laundry once the separate laundry had closed and there were no longer laundry maids. With better educational opportunities and higher expectations in post-war Britain, domestic service became a less popular choice of work. By the 1980s, only three staff remained at Brodsworth.

'This "upstairs downstairs" thing really irritates me. People talk about it as though it's happening now but it'd be going back to the First World War for all that nonsense. You definitely did not have any of that at Brodsworth. I mean, they had to work – poor souls – and we didn't, but apart from that …'
Pamela Grant-Dalton, speaking in 1993

Above: 'Miss Pam' photographed as a child, with Jane Langton, housekeeper, and the domestic staff
Right: The indoor servants photographed in 1914 by valet Alfred Edwards. His future wife, kitchen maid Caroline Palmer, is marked with a cross. Martha Lockey, cook, is second from left, and butler John Marshall is centre, standing behind Jane Langton, at that time a lady's maid

14 FIRST-FLOOR SERVANTS' WING

The entire first floor of the service wing provided accommodation for 13 female members of staff. At the head of the stairs was the housekeeper's bedroom and maids' sitting room, and in the adjacent corridor was a row of bells, replaced in about 1913 by an electric bell-board to summon them to any room in the house. Beyond a curtain across the corridor lay eight bedrooms, most of which were each shared by two maids. Halfway along this corridor is another huge linen cupboard for the servants' bedlinen; a linen list written by the housekeeper in 1873 is pasted inside one of its doors.

The bedrooms were spacious by comparison with the attic rooms usually allocated to servants in older country houses. They were comfortably furnished, with iron beds and painted or grained wooden wardrobes, chests of drawers and washstands with china wash-sets. Many of these survive, a reminder of their previous owners, but the carpets, bedding and curtains have disappeared, like the servants. By the 1950s, only four members of the Grant-Daltons' male and female staff used a small number of the rooms, which were redecorated at that time in an attempt to update them.

The maids' sitting room was originally furnished with chairs, crockery and a kettle. It was also where staff laundered and mended their own clothes. From the 1950s the room was used for ironing the items returned from the commercial laundry. The unused rooms became filled with objects no longer required in the rest of the house; there are several wooden washstands, made redundant once basins were plumbed in to the main bedrooms in the 1960s. Their jugs and bowls were often used thereafter to catch drips coming through ceilings around the house. These abandoned rooms, almost more than any others in the house, bear witness to the changes in the country-house way of life, once so dependent on plentiful and affordable staff.

15 LARDER AND KITCHEN

A staircase leads down to the main servants' offices, where the work required for supporting the family took place under the management of the butler, cook and housekeeper. Victorian country houses often had extensive service wings, with myriad rooms for different functions; Brodsworth's is relatively compact and well organized, incorporating the rear of the central section of the house, the cellars beneath and the ground floor of the adjoining lower block. Visitors first see the larder, a cool north-facing room with marble slabs, and food cupboards faced with gauze. A modern freezer replaced the lead-lined wooden refrigerator in the corridor outside, which had to be filled with ice. At the back of the larder, windows lend light to the housemaids' closet behind it. Once a store cupboard for

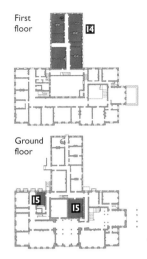

First floor

Ground floor

Above left: The maids' rooms now have an abandoned air
Below: The original kitchen

cleaning equipment, the space is now taken up by the lift-shaft.

The kitchen lies at the heart of the house and of the servants' wing. Its position near the dining room meant that food could be served while still hot, being taken by footmen from the hatch at the rear of the room. The kitchen's great height and louvred top-light meant it was both well lit and ventilated, with the maximum amount of space for work and fittings. In its early days the room would have been the scene of constant activity, as the cook, supported by two or three kitchen maids, produced meals with several courses for the family and their guests, as well as food for the servants themselves.

While most of the room's fittings date from the 1860s, some items were brought from the old hall, and there were minor repairs and replacements over the years. A major update took place in about 1910, possibly in preparation for the silver-wedding celebrations of Charles and Constance Mary Thellusson, for which a French chef was hired, the present Eagle range installed and many of the copper utensils with the initials 'CT' bought.

Above right: A rare photograph of staff at work in about 1909, recording Martha Lockey, cook from 1905 to 1915 on the left, and Caroline Palmer, kitchen maid, on the right
Below: The vast Eagle range dominates the room. It replaced the one hidden by the mobile warming cupboard in the earlier photograph

Cooking was transferred from here to the former still-room when there were no longer such large numbers of family or servants to cater for, probably during the 1920s under Augustus Thellusson, and certainly from the Grant-Daltons' time in the 1930s.

Apart from a brief period of use by the Army, when the house was requisitioned during the Second World War, the room and its contents were abandoned to gather rust and cobwebs; and unwanted or unwieldy items, such as ladders and

broken lamps, began to accumulate here. Its gentle conservation reveals both its former heyday and later abandonment.

16 BUTLER'S PANTRY

The butler's important role was emphasized by the position of this room, which gave him easy access both to the front door and to the corridors leading to the dining room and reception rooms, as well as to the rest of the service wing and the stairs to the cellars, where the wine and beer were stored. An electric bell-board nearby in the corridor let him know from which room a summons was being made.

The room was also used for the storage and cleaning of silver and glass, its tall cupboards being installed by Lapworths in 1863. Some of its contents, such as the linen for shooting parties and the wicker-covered bottles, demonstrate the fact that the family's outdoor pursuits and travels also required much preparation and work by the household servants. Brodsworth was rarely without a butler, and this room continued to be used into the 1980s.

17 SCULLERY

Opposite the kitchen is the scullery, where the hard and messy work of preparing meals and clearing up after them took place; this is why the position of scullery maid was the lowliest in the 19th-century household. There was once a large stone sink here for washing vegetables and dishes.

18 AGA KITCHEN

This room, with its cream-coloured Aga, Formica work surfaces added on to the Victorian table and cupboards and magnolia gloss paint on the walls, reflects how some of the changes in domestic work in the 20th century affected Brodsworth. When the house was built, this room was the still-room, where preserves and fancy desserts were made. With a reduced number of staff, it was more suitable for cooking than the original – by now outdated – kitchen. A cooker similar to this 1970s Aga replaced its small Victorian range at some point in the 1920s or 1930s.

For more than 40 years, this room was the domain of Emily Chester, who combined the role of cook and housekeeper from 1936 to 1981, spending her entire working life at Brodsworth

and building a close relationship with Sylvia Grant-Dalton. In a reversal of Victorian custom, Mrs Grant-Dalton used to come here every day to consult Emily about the day's menus. The strong smell of Mrs Grant-Dalton's coffee, ground especially each day, used to permeate this room, no matter what might be cooking on the range. Today, the smells and sounds of English Heritage's tea rooms come from further along the corridor. These were once the butler's and footmen's bedrooms, a gun-room and a store, and were converted into a flat for the butler in the 1960s.

The two large rooms each side of the door to the service yard were once the servants' dining hall and housekeeper's sitting room. The latter has an expanse of cupboards along one wall and was where linen and servants' crockery were stored.

19 SERVICE YARD

The service yard, now the tea terrace, would once have been extremely busy, with deliveries of produce arriving from the kitchen gardens and home farm, as well as from local shops and suppliers. There was also a well in the service yard, which provided a ready supply of fresh water.

Game was once stored in the game larder across the yard, while meat, vegetables, wine and beer were taken to the cellars (not open to visitors) down the steps that can be seen in the yard. Coal was also delivered into the cellars; from 1907 the coal used in the house was mined from the Brodsworth Main Colliery and carted over to the hall by the tenant farmers on 'coaling day'.

'I can always remember going in and seeing Emily behind that door … There she would be, sitting in the chair next to the Aga … And that kitchen always used to smell of ground coffee' Les Trott, estate foreman, recalling cook/housekeeper Emily Chester, above

Below: The Aga kitchen, with cook/housekeeper Emily Chester's chair close to the warmth of the range

Tour of the Gardens

Brodsworth Hall is surrounded by pleasure gardens extending to over 15 acres (6 hectares). These were laid out in the 1860s to provide a formal setting for Charles Sabine Augustus Thellusson's new house, and grounds that held plenty of interest and variety for the enjoyment of his family and guests. Beyond the spacious lawns immediately around the house lie a succession of flower and shrub beds, sculptural and architectural ornaments and meandering woodland walks. Paths with tunnels and bridges present enticing and ever-changing vistas.

The gardens had become very overgrown by 1990, but their original structure survived remarkably well. English Heritage has undertaken a careful restoration, aiming to recapture the original spirit of the gardens, while incorporating important later changes and new contributions such as national plant collections.

THE SETTING FOR THE HALL

In remodelling his estate, Charles Sabine Augustus Thellusson required a fashionably private garden setting for his new house, and productive kitchen gardens. It took the years between 1861 and 1868 and several thousands of pounds for all the building, landscaping, and planting to be complete. This work was undertaken by the first head gardener, Samuel Taylor, and the estate workforce of gardeners and woodmen, with a few specialist contractors. The gardens were typical of the mid-Victorian period, being very labour-intensive, with contrasting areas of formality, colourful planting, and dense shrubberies.

While Thellusson's vision dominates the gardens, elements from Brodsworth's earlier landscape can also be seen. As the drive leads through the outer woodland gardens, with their boundary of iron fencing and clipped evergreens, the vista suddenly opens out to reveal the house at the far side of an expanse of lawn. A cedar tree from the 18th-century gardens, and Brodsworth church nearby, lend a well-established air. The white limestone house is set off by the simple formality and matching Italianate style of the grounds immediately around it. Their 'green architecture' of lawns, terraces, and boundary hedge of clipped yew is punctuated by paths,

marble steps, urns and sculptures provided by the Italian sculptor Casentini in 1866. The long south front of the house, where all the principal rooms lie, looks out across a narrow terrace to the park, framed by woodland planted in the 18th century.

WEST LAWNS, FOUNTAIN GARDEN, SUMMER HOUSE AND PETS' CEMETERY

The formal lawns to the west of the house were often used for garden games such as croquet and tennis. A pair of wide shrub beds set with cedar trees and statues divides these lawns from a series

Top: The formal gardens at an early stage of their development, shortly after 1866
Above: The gravestone of the terrier Coup among those of other family dogs and Polly Parrot in the pets' cemetery
Left: The summer house closes the vista across the formal gardens

Facing page: The three-tiered Italian marble fountain supplied by Casentini in 1866

features in the gardens and many estate buildings. The man-made mound on which the summer house sits has been used as a tool store and at times an ice house in the days before refrigeration. A shallow rectangular depression in the park, just beyond the iron fence, could be flooded with water from a tank in the woods. Once frozen, the ice was cut and stored in the ice house. Former estate staff recall this practice in the 1930s, after which ice was collected from Doncaster in the estate van and stored in the house.

A path behind the summer house leads to the pets' cemetery where many of the family's dogs are buried. This tradition was started by Peter and Elizabeth Thellusson. The first dog to be buried here was one of their favourites, Coup, who died in 1894 and whose portrait by W H Trood can be seen in the morning room.

THE GROVE: ROCK GARDEN, GROTTO, TARGET HOUSE AND ROSE PERGOLA

A choice of paths lead from the summer house through a woodland area called the Grove. Winding walks here were part of the ornamental landscape surrounding the 18th-century house and made use of abandoned stone quarries. In the 1860s part of this area was made more ornate through specialized planting and rock

'There was a big bed of lily-of-the-valley. Mr Larner [head gardener] used to put them in, and we used to put frames over the top of them and grow them rather quickly and cut them in bunches and send them down to Covent Garden'
Joe Ward, gardener at Brodsworth, 1928 to 1934

of more intricately planted areas and woodland walks. The first and most elaborate of these areas, the fountain garden, has as its centrepiece the three-tiered marble fountain supplied by Casentini. Around it are geometric flower beds and four large tazzas or shallow urns, all of which provided an opportunity for head gardeners past and present to devise changing displays of brightly coloured bedding throughout the year.

The summer house, a small building in classical style, gives a vantage point from which to view the gardens and house. It was built in 1866 by the mason John Ball, as were most of the architectural

Above: Frederick Larner, seated centre in a boater, was head gardener from 1913 to 1940. About a dozen gardeners managed the pleasure and kitchen gardens until the 1930s
Right: The Grotto, replanted with ferns, with the summer house and eye-catcher beyond

Restoring the Gardens

Brodsworth's gardens were intended to be maintained by a team of gardeners, but these dwindled steadily in the second half of the 20th century. The outer parts of the gardens such as the Grove were abandoned to nature, flower and shrub borders became congested, and woodland encroached on the drives and garden buildings.

English Heritage was faced with very overgrown gardens in 1990. As the gardens could not be maintained in this state, and the framework of the original 1860s design was still evident, it was decided to restore them to their appearance at that date. Initial work concentrated on removing or reducing self-sown or over-mature trees and shrubs, re-establishing the general layout of paths and borders, and consolidating the garden buildings. Additional funding of £385,000 from the Heritage Lottery Fund over five years enabled considerable replanting, and the gardens now contain notable collections. The formal character and visual variety of the 1860s garden design is evident once again. As this restoration matures, elements from other points in the gardens' history, such as mid-20th century plantings and maturing trees, sit more easily.

The years of neglect have also left a legacy in the lawns with the evolution of the wild-flower meadow, which was not a feature of the Victorian gardens. Without close cutting and the use of herbicides, the lawns became rich in wild flowers such as cowslips, orchids and thyme. They are now a rare example in England of natural magnesian limestone grassland, which English Heritage is carefully conserving.

The gardens are also now home to plant collections that have been restored or introduced by English Heritage, including hollies, roses, ferns and alpines. Each element has its own history. The hollies were largely present when English Heritage took over, and responded well to the hard pruning necessary to restore their tightly clipped appearance. There are now more than 100 cultivars, all of them Victorian or earlier.

The rose collection was restored in the 1990s, using rose cultivars from the Victorian era or earlier. In a wooded dell, where wild roses were found, there are now 75 species of wild rose, with the potential to gain National Collection of Species Roses status. The fern collection was acquired from the widow of Wing Commander Eric Baker in 2000, after the British Fern Society identified the grotto as an ideal home for it.

The alpine collection was opened in 2008 near the summer house, making use of the Victorian drainage system of the rock garden. It consists of more than 200 alpines from all over the world.

'When I came here, I did my best to tidy things up, but it was more than one man's job. [Sylvia] didn't like cutting anything back. She used to like it to grow wild'
Bill Smith, gardener 1982–88 and the 1990s

Above: Sylvia Grant-Dalton in the rose pergola in the 1930s
Above left: Bill Smith, wearing a cap, working with English Heritage on the restoration of the gardens
Below, from far left: Rosa 'Comte de Chambord'; Rosa 'Mundi'; Leucanthemum vulgare; Anemone drummondii; Dodecatheon pulchellum

work. The first section of the rock garden faces towards the summer house, and has been replanted with alpine plants.

The path leads under a bridge to an enclosed area originally called the Grotto, installed by Joseph Barron in 1863 and 1864. The rock is arranged to form small pockets in order to create cascades of plants placed in crevices, with water piped to the cascade, and a 'river' of gravel traversed by stepping stones. The Grotto's structure has been restored and planted with ferns, a species popular in the Victorian period.

The maze of paths and bridges here offers a variety of views of the planting and architectural features which make these compact gardens seem twice their actual size. The use of angles, slopes and carefully located planting are designed to intrigue and draw visitors on to the next feature. At the back of the Grove is an eye-catcher, a deliberately created ruinous wall at one end of a long, straight expanse of grass. There are tightly winding paths and a herbaceous border on one side, and on the other borders are raised on 'spine banks'; these allow the planting to be seen to advantage and also created effective screens dividing the large, open quarry area into smaller sections. The grassed area, sometimes called the target range, ends at the Target House, the furthest point of the gardens where rests could be taken outside or in. Archery was a popular social activity for young ladies in the 19th century, and this little building was used to store equipment.

Bearing right from here, the planting predominantly of roses around an iron pergola has been much renewed, by both Mrs Grant-Dalton from the 1930s, and by English Heritage. From the paths through the woodland, glimpses can be gained of the estate buildings that served the hall – the home farm and its farmhouse, the estate office of 1913, the generator house, pump house and the 18th-century stable block. These buildings are not open to the public.

SITE OF OLD HALL AND FORMER KITCHEN GARDENS

The 18th-century Brodsworth Hall lay between the stables and the church, just beyond the boundary fence at the bottom of the children's adventure playground. The north drive runs from the new hall towards the church, where it leaves

English Heritage's property. Curving round the site of the old house, the drive led to the stables, home farm and laundry, with a track to the right leading to the kitchen gardens. This must once have been one of the busiest routes on the estate.

The extensive walled kitchen gardens had been established in the 18th century, but they were substantially altered for Charles Sabine Augustus Thellusson in 1862–3. Additional glasshouses were built to grow exotic fruit, vegetables and flowers, including vines, peaches, figs and mushrooms, and a spring conduit built to provide a constant water supply. Serried ranks of fruit and vegetables were grown throughout the

garden for use by the family and staff of the hall, and some produce was sold commercially from the 1890s. The head gardener's house stood at one end of the gardens, and a bothy accommodated young unmarried gardeners near the glasshouses. With fewer garden staff and a smaller family at the hall in the mid-20th century, the kitchen gardens were let out commercially from the early 1940s to the late 1960s. At this point Mr and Mrs Williams (Pamela) moved in to the former head gardener's house, creating an ornamental garden around it. The glasshouses were demolished and the lower half of the kitchen gardens became pasture. The kitchen gardens are private property and are not accessible to visitors.

The church of St Michael and All Angels, which features Saxon and Norman stonework, once stood out prominently on the ridge above the village of Brodsworth. The entire area was much landscaped by Charles Sabine Augustus Thellusson, with banks reshaped, trees planted and the churchyard reduced in size. The result is that the church now appears to be in a secluded area of woodland at the corner of the gardens, almost like a private chapel. Indeed, among other restoration work to the church that Thellusson commissioned in 1877, he also built a new aisle to accommodate his family and staff more comfortably. St Michael and All Angels is still in use, one of four churches in a united benefice. It lies outside English Heritage's property, but is occasionally opened to visitors by volunteers on summer Sundays.

Right: The summer house engulfed by trees in 1994
Below: The geometric shapes and brilliant colours of the beds in the fountain garden draw on mid-Victorian published designs. Their planting changes twice a year

The Brodsworth Estate

Brodsworth Hall and its gardens were once the heart of a large agricultural estate. When English Heritage took on the hall in 1990, the estate was retained in family ownership.

An estate provided not only the aesthetic setting for a country house, but financial support in rental incomes and agricultural produce, and a resident labour force. Brodsworth was one of a series of gentlemen's estates which had been developed on the fertile farmland of the limestone ridge to the west of Doncaster by the 17th and 18th centuries. Much of the work undertaken by the eighth earl of Kinnoull and subsequently his son, the archbishop of York, during the 18th century to fashion Brodsworth into an impressive country seat has been swept away by later developments. Traces of it survive, however, in the stables, the outline of the kitchen gardens, and the narrow woodland bordering the park, which is all that remains of the former Brodsworth Wood.

Charles Sabine Augustus Thellusson's remodelling of his estate of 8,000 acres (3,240 hectares) in the 1860s gave it a structure still visible today. The new hall was sited away from the village, its park enlarged by the removal of old field boundaries. He modernized the stables, formed a laundry from the old brewhouse, and built new farmhouses, cottages and a school, giving Brodsworth and Pickburn the character of estate villages. Farms were improved with efficiently laid-out new buildings. The woods were rejuvenated and a team of nine gamekeepers employed to manage pheasant and partridge shooting. The Thellussons' way of life required the support of the entire estate community, for whom the estate provided homes, workplaces, education and social care in return. The estate accounts reveal that whole families were directly employed in the house, gardens and woods, and as craftsmen such as masons and carpenters, while others were employed by the tenant farmers.

The estate was profoundly affected by the changing circumstances of the late 19th and 20th centuries. As agricultural incomes fell, the estate's timber and mineral resources were exploited. The lease of land to the Brodsworth Main Colliery in 1905 brought new income, but also huge physical changes to the estate landscape with industrial buildings and the new model village of Woodlands. The additional income did, however, allow Charles Thellusson to indulge his personal interest in breeding pedigree cattle and poultry.

The character and way of life of Brodsworth's paternalistic Victorian estate gradually faded during the 20th century. The number of people employed on the estate fell, particularly with the mechanisation of agriculture. Buildings and land were sold over the years, including for nearby commercial and motorway developments. The estate of some 4,000 acres (1,619 hectares) is now managed by the Williams family trustees.

Although the Hall and gardens have been managed separately from the estate as a heritage attraction since 1990, the parkland and estate buildings continue to provide an impressive physical setting and a reminder of the once important role of the Brodsworth estate.

'My dad worked all his life on Brodsworth estate, apart from two years at Brodsworth Colliery during the war. Brodsworth Church, his work and his family had been his life. He'd hardly left the village … Well, you didn't in those days, did you?'
Margaret Handley recalls her father, Reginald Taylor, estate worker from 1927 to the 1980s

Above: Reginald Taylor on his wedding to Brodsworth housemaid Kathleen Fenn in 1939
Above left: William Chesher, head herdsman, with a prize Jersey bull at the 'model' dairy farm created in 1910
Left: The head gardener's house and kitchen gardens in the early 20th century. Fruit, vegetables and flowers for cutting were grown in a series of beds and glasshouses

History of Brodsworth

From the time of the Norman Conquest onwards, a series of families built up a substantial landholding at Brodsworth. In the early 18th century, Brodsworth became one of the seats of the eighth earl of Kinnoull, and for a time was home to the archbishop of York, one of the earl's sons. Then in 1791 Brodsworth was sold to a banker, Peter Thellusson. The terms of his notorious will put the estate, after five decades of legal wrangling, into the hands of the man who created the house and gardens we see today.

EARLY HISTORY

The modern Brodsworth estate lies within an area which has been settled since at least the late Iron Age. By the middle of the 11th century there was a manor house and church here, owing allegiance to the minster church at Conisbrough. Extensive earthworks about 100m east of the church of St Michael and All Angels mark the original location of Brodsworth village. After the Conquest of 1066, the estate, comprising Brodsworth, Pickburn and Scawsby, passed from its Saxon owner Alsi to the Norman knight Roger de Busli. During the reign of Henry I (r.1100–1135) it was given to William de Orrell, or Darrell, in recognition of his support for the king against rebellious Scots and Yorkshiremen. The Darrell family, whose principal seat was Sessay in north Yorkshire, held the estate until 1505, when Sir John Darrell died without issue and was succeeded by his sister Joan, wife of Sir Guy Dawnay of Cowick, 12 miles to the north.

The Brodsworth estate remained with the Dawnays until the beginning of the 17th century, when it came into the hands of the Wentworths of nearby North Elmsall. Darcy Wentworth, the first member of the family known to have lived at Brodsworth, played an important role in the English Civil War on the Parliamentary side. On one occasion he was captured by the Royalists, condemned to be shot and was tied to a stake; but he managed to barter his release, and went on to die quietly in his bed in 1667.

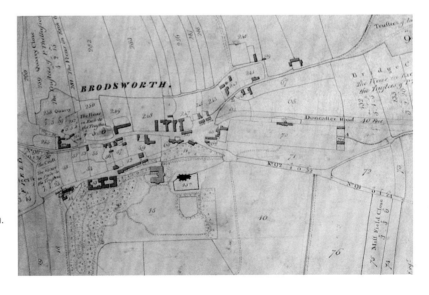

Above: Robert Hay Drummond (1711–76), archbishop of York, improved the old Brodsworth Hall and its estate in the 18th century
Below: The short south front of the old Brodsworth Hall overlooking the park, photographed before its demolition in 1861

After Darcy's death Brodsworth passed to Henry, the second son of Darcy's nephew, Sir Thomas Wentworth of North Elmsall. After Henry's death, Brodsworth appears to have been used as a dower house for his widow, Susan, until 1702 and was then leased out to a distant relation, Godfrey Wentworth, who paid £35 a year for the house, gardens and grounds. Surviving estate accounts from this period reveal minor repairs to the house but give little clue as to its character, though it was probably rather modest.

THE EARLS OF KINNOULL

In 1713 Henry's son Sir John Wentworth sold the house and estate to George Hay, viscount Dupplin, eldest son and heir to Thomas, seventh earl of Kinnoull, who was looking for a country seat where he might pass his time 'in a very private manner at a distance from all public affairs'. Dupplin, who had recently fallen from political favour, was arrested in 1715 on suspicion of having Jacobite sympathies. When released a year later he retired to Brodsworth, devoting his energies to the management of the estate. The house was probably rebuilt during this period, the gardens and parkland laid out and the estate extended. Heavy losses in the South Sea Bubble financial crisis of 1720 must have brought work to an end as the by now eighth earl of Kinnoull was left close to bankruptcy. Leaving his wife and many children to fend for themselves at Brodsworth, he now spent most of his time in London, and from

1729 to 1736 served as British ambassador to the Sublime Porte in Constantinople, a posting from which he was recalled by the king in disgrace because of his poor judgement of character and fondness for drink. Surviving estate accounts from 1730 show that the countess derived only £700 a year rental income from the estate during this period, barely enough to support her family of ten children comfortably.

The eighth earl of Kinnoull died in 1758 and was succeeded by his eldest son, Thomas, but it was the second son, Robert Hay Drummond, who came to live at Brodsworth on his appointment as archbishop of York in 1761. The archbishop divided his time between Brodsworth, for which he had a lifelong affection, and the archbishop's palace at Bishopthorpe, just south of York, and carried out extensive improvements to both. Brodsworth was remodelled in the 1770s, perhaps by Robert Adam, who supplied eight drawings for a major rebuilding in 1768. Work was certainly under way by 1775, when a correspondent noted that Drummond was 'very busy building new rooms & an elegant front to the south'. The results, seen in photographs of the old hall, were very different to Adam's drawings. They show a hipped roof and bays on the south and east façades, features suggestive of a mid-18th-century date. This period was the social high point in the history of the house, when such figures as the duke of Portland and Lord Rockingham were regular visitors.

After the archbishop's death in 1777 the estate fell into neglect. His elder brother, Thomas, the ninth earl, had retired to Dupplin Castle in Perthshire and showed little interest in his English estates. When he died in 1787 his title and lands passed to Robert Auriol, eldest son of the archbishop, who became tenth earl of Kinnoull. An inventory taken at the time reveals that the house had seven bedchambers, two drawing rooms, two dining rooms, a hall, library and study. The tenth earl sold the Brodsworth estate in 1791.

THE THELLUSSONS

Peter Thellusson, who purchased the Brodsworth estate, came from a family long established in European commerce. As Huguenots (French Protestants) the Thellussons had fled religious persecution on more than one occasion, but flourished through widespread business and

family contacts. The Thellussons were velvet manufacturers near Lyons in the 16th century, and subsequently merchants and financiers principally in France and then in Geneva. Isaac de Thellusson (1690–1755) re-established the family's financial business in Paris in 1715, becoming a major lender to Louis XV and Geneva's representative at the French court in the 1730s.

PETER THELLUSSON

The youngest of Isaac Thellusson's sons, Pierre, later known as Peter (1735–97), established himself in London in 1760, becoming part of the Huguenot commercial community there. He immediately became a British citizen by act of Parliament in 1760. The following year, he married an Englishwoman, Anne Woodford, from a minor gentry family with Lincolnshire roots.

Peter Thellusson built up a fortune as a merchant and a banker, providing credit and insurance, particularly for ships and their cargoes, some of which he part-owned. Many of his commercial activities related to the West Indian sugar trade, which was reliant on the African slave trade. He owned sugar warehouses in London, and through loans to plantation owners who subsequently defaulted, he also became an

absentee owner of plantations and slaves in Grenada and Montserrat. Peter Thellusson was sufficiently prosperous to invest in land. He built a Palladian villa at then-rural Plaistow near Bromley in Kent in the 1770s, and made the prestigious purchase of the Brodsworth estate in 1791. After a career of more than 30 years Thellusson gradually retired from business and died in 1797, choosing to be buried at Brodsworth.

*Above: Charles Thellusson
(1791–1856)*
*Below: Rataplan, Charles
Thellusson's racehorse,
painted by Harry Hall
(1815–82) on winning the
Doncaster Cup in 1855*

PETER THELLUSSON'S WILL

The peculiar nature of Peter Thellusson's will of 1796 meant that all his property, including the Brodsworth estate, was to be managed by trustees for the 60 years following his death. The will caused an immediate and long-lasting sensation because its unusual terms had the potential to create fabulous wealth at an unspecified future time. It was feared that this could be economically and socially destabilizing, and a law was swiftly passed to prevent such a thing happening again, the 1800 Accumulations Act, or the 'Thellusson Act'.

In the will, Peter Thellusson left £100,000 to his three sons, who were by then seeking advancement through Parliament and the peerage. This sum he considered 'sufficient to procure them comfort'. The eldest, Peter, was created Baron Rendlesham in 1806. The bulk of the fortune, some £600,000 (about £33.6m today) in land and investments was left to accumulate for future generations. It could be inherited only on the death of the last of Peter Thellusson's sons or grandsons who were alive at the time of his death. The final settlement was eventually triggered in 1856 by the death of Charles Sabine Augustus Thellusson's father, also called Charles.

Peter Thellusson's sons attempted unsuccessfully to overturn the will, with the result that the estate was put into the Court of Chancery. The terminology of the will was also disputed, particularly the phrase that defined who would eventually inherit: 'the eldest male lineal descendants of my three sons then living'. If there were none, the fortune was to help pay the National Debt.

The final legal judgement came in 1858, when the inheritance was divided between two people, Frederick, the fourth Lord Rendlesham; and Charles Sabine Augustus Thellusson (1822–85), whose portion included the Brodsworth estate.

The will was also infamous for keeping the legal profession profitably employed for a long time, fighting the numerous cases and managing the estate in Chancery. The Thellusson will has been claimed as the inspiration for Charles Dickens's depiction of the all-devouring legal world in *Bleak House*. Dickens, however, never confirmed this, and there were several other protracted Chancery cases upon which he could have drawn for the novel.

THE TRUSTEES' PERIOD

During the period governed by the will, Peter Thellusson's trustees continued to buy land, as he had instructed, while benefiting considerably in person. The courts attempted to rectify this situation in 1835, reprimanding the luxurious life enjoyed at Brodsworth by one trustee, Sir Charles Flint, and allowing the Thellusson family to receive rents from the Thellusson estates.

Although Peter Thellusson's sons could not fully enjoy his properties, his youngest son, Charles (1770–1815), did spend time at Brodsworth, where he is buried. His son, also Charles (1797–1856), seen as the little boy in red in the portrait by Lawrence (page 36), flitted restlessly about Europe before settling in Worthing, unable to extract money from the trust even for the education of his son, Charles Sabine Augustus Thellusson, one of the will's likely beneficiaries. Charles Thellusson's passion was the turf. One of his acquaintances was John Theobald, who had built up the largest commercial racing stud in England from the profits of his hosiery business. Theobald's granddaughter, Georgiana, married Charles Sabine Augustus Thellusson in 1850, and the trophies and paintings of racehorses at Brodsworth today are reminders of this connection.

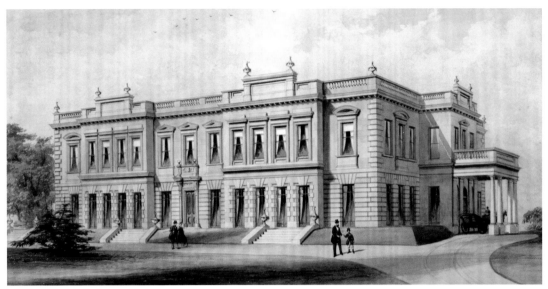

Above: Charles Sabine Augustus Thellusson at about the time the house was built in 1863
Left: A watercolour, possibly by the architect Philip Wilkinson, to illustrate the proposed new house
Below: A portrait of Charles Sabine Augustus Thellusson as a captain in the 12th Royal Lancers in about 1848, attributed to Alfred Courbould (1831–75)

Charles Sabine Augustus Thellusson had, therefore, been brought up with 'great expectations', and before his marriage he spent a few years in a fashionable regiment. Georgiana's wealth, augmented by the deaths in quick succession of her grandfather and father, enabled the couple to rent Marlborough House, one of the most prestigious addresses in Brighton, for the first ten years of their marriage. All of their six children were born there, and Thellusson could afford to indulge in the fashionable sport of yachting along the south coast.

THE INHERITANCE AND NEW HOUSE

When Charles Sabine Augustus Thellusson came into his inheritance, he had at last attained the wealth and station in life to which his father had so long aspired. By selling off some of his inherited funds and land holdings elsewhere, he was able to consolidate Brodsworth into a model country seat with a large agricultural and sporting estate centred on a fashionable house and gardens.

The creation of new country houses and the alteration of old ones was at a peak in the 1860s. Thellusson was one of many who had the confidence to pull down an existing house and build afresh. He followed the fairly common practice by that date of using a London architect to produce a full specification, and building contractors working to a strict contract, with a fixed price and time limit. It was an impressive achievement that, with plans for the new house drawn up in 1861, the house had

been roofed and furnished by 1863, at a cost of just over £45,000.

Brodsworth Hall was the chief work of the little-known architect Philip Wilkinson, who is otherwise credited with designing housing in London. Thellusson's use of Wilkinson and the London contractor Longmire and Burge, together with the Bond Street furnishing firm Lapworths, brought him metropolitan quality with a certain economy. Wilkinson's well-proportioned Italianate house reused materials from the old house and stone quarried on the estate, combined with luxurious materials, such as scagliola and marble, and hand-painted surfaces. With its Minton tiles

*Above: Peter Thellusson
(1850–99), Charles Sabine
Augustus Thellusson's
eldest son*

*Above right: Elizabeth
St Clair McDougall in the
late 1870s, when she was a
companion to the Thellusson
girls, photographed by
Peter Thellusson, whom she
was later to marry*

*Below: Constance Thellusson
and Horace Grant-Dalton's
wedding party on the
south terrace in June 1883*

and machine-made and hand-knotted carpets, the house is as much the product of the era of the railway and industrial production as of individual craftsmen.

Work in the grounds continued for several more years under the direction of the head gardener and head woodman, with the gardens being laid out, the parkland extended, and the woodlands renovated. Longmire and Burge had further contracts in the 1860s and 1870s for new approach roads and houses for the head gardener and gamekeeper, while other estate buildings were constructed by local building firms. In a period of intense activity and investment, Thellusson had turned his somewhat neglected estate into a seat suitable for a sporting gentleman. His acceptance

into the ranks of the Yorkshire gentry was marked by his appointment as high sheriff for the West Riding in 1865. This position was later filled by his son, Charles, and grandson, Charles Grant-Dalton, while his sons Peter and Herbert both served as justices of the peace. None of the family gained influence beyond the locality.

THE NEXT GENERATION: THELLUSSON'S CHILDREN

When Charles Sabine Augustus and Georgiana Thellusson moved from Brighton up to their new house at Brodsworth in 1863, their six children ranged in age from the thirteen-year-old Peter to Augustus, a new baby. Their staff included nursemaids and a governess, mainly for the two girls who were educated at home. The boys attended schools in Brighton and then Eton for brief periods, and all developed a life-long passion for their father's favourite sports of shooting and sailing. Peter was at Oxford University briefly and travelled abroad. The celebrations in 1872 for his coming of age, as heir to the estate, were a major event at Brodsworth, with three days of entertainments laid on for family, friends, the estate tenantry and workforce.

The early 1880s saw fundamental changes to the structure of the family. Aline, the elder daughter, died of a lung complaint in 1880 at the age of 24. Georgiana died in 1883 after many years of ill health, a few months before the wedding at Brodsworth of her younger daughter, Constance, to Horace Grant-Dalton, a distant relation from Somerset. Later the same year Peter married Elizabeth St Clair McDougall. She had been his sisters' governess in the 1860s and then a companion to them and their mother, a position that had suddenly become redundant as a result of of the two deaths and Constance's marriage.

The year 1885 was another significant one for the family. Charles Sabine Augustus Thellusson died in March, shortly before the weddings of two of his other sons. Herbert, after a short but extravagant army career, married a rich young widow, also from Somerset, Sarah Greenhill. Charles married Constance Mary Philips, one of the daughters of the vicar of Brodsworth. The youngest son, Augustus, remained a bachelor. The only one of all the marriages to

Sporting Interests

Sport was an important ingredient in the lives of several generations of Thellussons. Charles Thellusson (d.1856) was a keen follower of racing and owned the horse Rataplan, but equestrian sports were not the primary interest of other members of the family. His son, Charles Sabine Augustus Thellusson, became a major figure in British yachting, commissioning innovative and successful sailing yachts, including the fastest and largest of their day. The *Aline*, commissioned in 1860, a year before the new Brodsworth Hall, won Thellusson the Queen's Cup. It also established the career of its designer, Ben Nicholson, of the renowned yacht-builder Camper & Nicholsons. Thellusson was Commodore of the Royal Victoria Yacht Club on the Isle of Wight, and continued to commission and race new yachts, taking the family to the south coast each summer. His sons also commissioned yachts, but preferred steam-power to sail. Charles Thellusson (d.1919) often took parties on his steam yacht *Carmela* to Norway or Scotland for the salmon fishing. Charles Grant-Dalton was also a keen sailor, running a series of motor yachts, including the *Sylvia*.

Charles Sabine Augustus Thellusson's favourite winter sport was shooting. He employed eight to ten gamekeepers to ensure excellent pheasant and partridge shooting across the estate. Country-house life at this period often revolved around shooting parties, and Brodsworth's game books record the large quantities of game shot by family members both on their own and when entertaining. From the 1870s, game, and particularly rabbits, were sold, but made only a small contribution to the high costs of the sport. Charles Sabine Thellusson's four sons were brought up to enjoy shooting and kept it up on this scale into the 1920s, even during the First World War. Charles Grant-Dalton eventually let the shooting out to a syndicate in the 1930s to share its costs. Shooting continues at Brodsworth, although it plays only a small part in estate activities.

Left: The Aline, photographed in about 1860 by Jabez Hughes of Ryde. This influential and successful racing yacht was later owned by the Prince of Wales
Below left: Constance Mary Thellusson in Norway in about 1909
Below centre: The valet Alfred Edwards loading the guns for Charles Thellusson in about 1915
Below right: Charles Sabine Augustus Thellusson in about 1874–80, on board his schooner Boadicea, built by Camper & Nicholsons. At 380 tons, it was the largest pure sailing yacht ever built in this country

Right: Brodsworth Main Colliery in 1907, the year in which coal was first brought to the surface
Below: Charles and Constance Mary Thellusson on the west lawn during their silver-wedding celebrations in 1910

produce children was that of Constance, so it was to be her elder son, Charles Grant-Dalton, who eventually inherited the estate in 1931.

THE BRODSWORTH COLLIERY

After his father's death, Peter Thellusson had to undertake major repairs to the house and estate buildings immediately. He and Elizabeth also introduced new furnishings, including oriental rugs and textiles, from shops such as Liberty and Maples. Their way of life and the number of staff altered

little, but it became increasingly difficult to keep change at bay. Income from the estate had been falling, as agriculture went into depression throughout the country at the end of the 19th century. The possibility of generating extra income from mineral reserves was first mooted in the 1890s by Peter's land agent, but it was not until 1905 that Charles Thellusson leased land to the newly formed Brodsworth Colliery Company. This brought income from rent and royalties on the coal mined, until the nationalisation of the coal industry in 1947. Brodsworth Main Colliery became one of the most productive in the country, but was closed in 1992. The pit tip that once dominated the skyline near the estate village of Pickburn has now been landscaped as a woodland for the use of the public.

The additional income from coal helped Charles to live a comfortable life as the squire of Brodsworth in the first two decades of the 20th century, entertaining and making many yachting trips, particularly for the fishing off Norway and Scotland. From 1908 he replaced his horse-drawn carriages with some of Britain's earliest cars. He and his wife Constance Mary renewed the decoration of several rooms, updated the kitchen, and introduced electricity to replace gas in 1913.

THE FIRST WORLD WAR

The 1914–18 war took many of Brodsworth's employees away from the estate, and female servants began to take on the work of the absent men in the gardens and on the wider estate. Staff numbers did not recover after the war, and increasingly, servants began to have a broader, less well-defined range of duties, often combining roles that would previously have been separate. The reduction in staff, however, had relatively little effect on Charles Thellusson's way of life. He died a year after the war ended, and his widow moved back to Torquay, where their married life had started. She died there in 1946.

By the time that Augustus Thellusson inherited the estate in 1919 at the age of 56, he had long been settled at Broadstairs in Kent. Although increasingly afflicted by gout, he came to his childhood home of Brodsworth for the shooting each winter during the 1920s. This meant that the house and gardens were managed by a relatively small staff, but the number of gamekeepers was always kept high.

THE GRANT-DALTONS

In 1931 Charles Grant-Dalton inherited an estate which he had known all his life. He and his brother Stuart spent a great deal of their youth at Brodsworth, particularly after the deaths at a young age of their parents, Constance (née Thellusson) and Horace Grant-Dalton. They were among the young relations, with Molly and Adeline Thellusson (pictured on the frontispiece), much welcomed by the hospitable but childless Charles and Constance Thellusson.

Both Charles and Stuart Grant-Dalton served in the First World War, and in 1916 Charles married the young Sylvia West, whose family were part of the Thellussons' circle of friends on the south coast. After the war Charles and Sylvia Grant-Dalton settled on the Hampshire coast near Lymington, where their only child, Pamela, was brought up. She was 11 when the family came to live at Brodsworth in 1931, which brought a child and governess into the hall again after many years.

Charles Grant-Dalton followed the footsteps of his Thellusson forebears at Brodsworth and was very much the squire; the hall was often used for entertaining, with several hunt balls being held during the 1930s. Pamela and Sylvia were presented at court in 1939, and Charles was high sheriff of West Yorkshire in 1943. The family spent most summers at their house at Quinnish on the Isle of Mull, as Charles was a keen sailor.

Charles Grant-Dalton did, however, feel the financial pressures now affecting landowners. Death duties in the 1930s forced him to sell paintings and a portion of the estate at Marr nearby. He leased

Left: Sylvia Grant-Dalton and her daughter Pamela, with ostrich-feather headdresses for their presentation at Court in 1939
Below: Charles and Pamela Grant-Dalton enjoying the snow to the north of the main drive in the park. The glasshouses in the kitchen garden can be seen beyond

out Brodsworth's shooting rights, and after 1941 the kitchen gardens were let commercially. The Grant-Daltons made the hall more comfortable and up-to-date, but they also adapted furnishings economically from one room to suit another, and reduced the number of rooms they used.

THE SECOND WORLD WAR

Brodsworth was requisitioned for military use in June 1940 following the evacuation of the army from Dunkirk. The exhausted soldiers arrived at Brodsworth days later and were billeted across the estate, some camping in the park. The Hall initially became the headquarters for General Arthur Percival of the 44th (Home Counties) Infantry

Fewer people were employed in the house and on the estate: while there had been six live-in staff at Brodsworth before the war, by the 1960s there were only a butler and the long-serving cook-housekeeper, Emily Chester, supported by some casual labour. Mrs Grant-Dalton struggled to replace employees whenever they left, relying increasingly on daily help ('dailies') and workers employed on a casual basis. Even the conversion of the valet and footmen's rooms into a butler's flat eventually failed to retain staff for long.

SYLVIA GRANT-DALTON

After Charles Grant-Dalton's death in 1952, the estate was left in trust for his daughter, Pamela. His widow Sylvia continued to live at the hall as a life-tenant, having the companionship of a second marriage from 1959 to 1970 to Eustace Grant-Dalton, one of Charles's cousins. Eustace, who had had a distinguished military career, had also known Brodsworth since his youth.

Mrs Grant-Dalton is remembered as a redoubtable, energetic person, taking an interest in every detail of the estate and its families, as well as the many other local causes with which she was involved. She continued to maintain the hall to the best of her ability in difficult circumstances, supported by ever fewer staff. Emily Chester, only a year older than her employer, remained with her until 1981, when at the age of 83 she completed a remarkable 71 years of service.

Above: Sylvia Grant-Dalton in the upstairs sitting room. Originally the day nursery, this spacious room over the main entrance was used as a sitting room from the early 20th century

Right: Sylvia (seated, second from left) and Pamela Grant-Dalton (standing, second from right) volunteered at the Warde-Aldam hospital at Frickley during the Second World War

Below: Stuart Grant-Dalton (1886–1971) served with distinction in the Royal Flying Corps in the First World War. He was awarded a bar to his DSO after the action in which he lost his leg

Division, who organized home defence, and was then used throughout the war by a series of army units undertaking training. The family were restricted to a few rooms, while the dining room became the officers' mess and army cooks took over the old kitchen. There was a Royal Signals office in the servants' wing, and the home farm was used as a NAAFI with a cookhouse and entertainment room. Charles Grant-Dalton commanded the local Home Guard, while Sylvia and Pamela both nursed. Pamela also served in the Air Transport Auxiliary.

The post-war period saw many changes for Brodsworth, as for other country-house estates.

In Service at Brodsworth

Louie Walton, née Nicholson, 1914–2009, was a housemaid at Brodsworth in the late 1930s, until she left to get married. When Louie worked at Brodsworth, the number of indoor staff had been reduced to six, down from about 15 in the hall's Victorian and Edwardian heyday

'There was six of us: Peggy the kitchen maid, Emily the housemaid, Kathleen the parlourmaid, Gladys the under-housemaid, John Parsons the butler, and me. We all slept in. Two women used to come in in the mornings, Mrs Simpson and Mrs Colledge. John Parsons was a nice man. He was single and used to go with the family when they were on the yacht all summer.

'When I first got up, I used to have the fire nicely red and burned through in the sitting room [the former day nursery] for when they came in before going down to breakfast at nine o'clock. Then I'd do their bedroom and the other bedrooms and that corridor. I don't know, but I was always busy doing something.

'Mr Larner, the head gardener, used to put the flowers in the sitting room. There was a great big mirror on the wall and a trough along the bottom of it, which he used to fill with flowers. It looked beautiful because the mirror reflected it. There was a plain red carpet and two cages with a parrot and two parakeets in that used to scratch the sand and shake themselves and all their feathers used to come out on to the floor. I used to Hoover that carpet five or six times a day.

'When they were on the boat, the family left the dogs at home, and after we had our lunch, we girls used to take the dogs for a walk in the grounds.

'When Kathleen was off I had to help in the dining room. I once went in with a new pair of shoes on. Next morning, Mrs Grant-Dalton – it's the only time she ever pulled me up – said: "Louie, you mustn't go in the dining room with squeaky shoes." I said, "Well, my others are shabby," and she said, "Well, wear your shabby ones then."

'One time Miss Pam was there on holiday and said, "Louie, I've caught my heel on the hem of my skirt – will you sew it for me?" She didn't know her mother was there, and Mrs Grant-Dalton said, "Pamela, did they teach you to sew at school?" Pamela said, "Yes," and Mrs Grant-Dalton replied, "I have Louie to look after me, and you

sew that yourself." So she told her off. She was nice, Miss Pam, though. She had charm.

'I slept in the first room past the bathroom. In the servants' bedrooms there was no heating, and we were in cotton sheets all winter. It was cold. And we had to get washed in cold water as well. There was no place for us to relax, really. I had a quarter of an hour or so in my own bedroom when I used to go up to get washed before I put my black afternoon frock on. I don't know why you had to change your uniform before dinner, because I never saw anybody. But that was the rule.

'They didn't entertain a lot. Apart from Miss Pam, who came from school once and brought a friend, the only visitors we had were Captain Grant-Dalton's brother, who was a wing commander, and his wife. I had to take morning tea into them. The first morning, I knocked and the wing commander said, "Come in." I took the tea in and I stood, flabbergasted. He says, "It's alright, Louie, it won't hurt you." There was a false leg stood up by the side of the bed. I'd never seen one as big, right up to the thigh it was, full leg.'

> 'The first morning, I knocked and the wing commander, Captain Grant-Dalton's brother, said, "Come in." I took the tea in, and I stood, flabbergasted.'

Above: *Louie Walton, at about the time of her wedding in 1938*
Left: *Peeling potatoes in the sun at Brodsworth's back door; housemaid Gladys Phillips is sitting on the right, Kathleen Fenn on the left, and Emily Chester is drying up*

BRODSWORTH TODAY

Mrs Grant-Dalton felt a strong duty to preserve the hall and strove to secure its future when it became clear that her daughter did not wish to live in it. Pamela had married Ronald Williams in 1958, and after some years in Gibraltar, where he was Commissioner of Police, they returned to live at Brodsworth, but chose to be in the more manageable and comfortable head gardener's house.

Mr and Mrs Williams both took an active interest in the estate, and, following Mrs Grant-Dalton's death in 1988, decided to retain the estate but not the hall. It took two years for negotiations to be completed to secure the hall's transfer to English Heritage. Pamela died in 1994, and since Ronald Williams's death in 2001, the estate has been managed by trustees for his family.

Pamela Williams gave Brodsworth Hall and its gardens to English Heritage in 1990. The National Heritage Memorial Fund purchased its contents for £3.36m, and English Heritage spent a matching sum on all the work required to conserve the property and open it to the public in 1995. The conservation, restoration and maintenance work continues, to ensure that Brodsworth Hall and its gardens will be enjoyed in the future, and tell their tale of aspiration, adaptation and survival.